DRIVE

DRIVE

poems by

Nadell Fishman

BROWN PEPPER PRESS
MONTPELIER VERMONT

Library of Congress Cataloging-in-Publication Data

Fishman, Nadell, 1953–
    Drive: poems / by Nadell Fishman.
      p.   cm.
    ISBN 0-9703090-0-7 (pbk.)
      I. Title.

    PS3556.I814573 D75 2000
    811'.6—dc21   00-051895

Printed in the United States.

Brown Pepper Press
P.O. Box 1030
Montpelier, VT 05601

Book design by Kate Mueller
Book Production by Electric Dragon Productions, Montpelier, Vermont
Logo artwork by Heidi Broner

Grateful acknowledgment to the editors of the following magazines in which these poems first appeared: *Fiction International* ("Study"); *Tendril* ("The Covenant"); *25% Rag* ("Throwing Wood"); *Calliope,* Roger Williams College ("Garden"); *The American Journal of Art Therapy* ("Woman in Clay"); *Bridges* ("Planting"); *The Burning World* ("Seven Beauties," "Storm"); *The Montpelier Bridge* ("Yarn," "Winter Blooms"); and *Writers Hotel* ("Test," "Tableau with Beautiful Women and Weights," "Elevator to the Stars").

"Garden" also appeared in the Beacon Press anthology *Her Face in the Mirror: Jewish Women on Mothers and Daughters,* edited by Faye Moskowitz, 1994.

Some of these poems appeared in *Seven Beauties,* a chapbook published by Norwich University Press, 1994.

Acknowledgments

I'm blessed to be part of a community of writer friends who have met regularly since 1988. My love and thankfulness to Judith Chalmer, Diane Swan, Charlie Barasch, Valerie Koropatnik, Francette Cerulli, Marian Willmott, Christine Korfhage, and past members Scudder Parker, Arthur Stone, Nicola Morris, and Linda Davies. Thanks to members of that first workshop, Linda McCarriston, Sherry Olson, Kit Gates, Susan Squier, Michael Carrino, and Paul Laffal.

Three times a year for the past decade, I've been fortunate to be part of the Writers Hotel. Grateful thanks to Tom Absher, our leader, for reading and offering thoughtful commentary on several variations of this manuscript, and thanks also to Sarah Hooker, Jane Bryant, David Rees, Bill Gazzola, Erika Butler, Wendy Willard, Sue Gleason, Steve Swanson, Jan Melampy, Alec Hastings, Peter Hendrick, Ernie Dodge, Peg Parke, and past members of the Writers Hotel.

More thanks to these dear friends, both writer and not, who have been generous readers: Teil Silverstein, Wendy Stevens, Spencer Smith, Jane Shore, Rhoda Carroll, Geof Hewitt, Margaret Harmon, and Dianne Maccario.

Special thanks to Jane Bryant, Spencer Smith, and Charlie Barasch for their editorial assistance with this book. And thanks to Cynthia Price, who generously provided the painting that graces the cover of *Drive*.

Blessings to my original first reader, my sister Dina Wilcox. And my love and gratitude to my husband, Andrew Kline, who, among other things, isn't afraid to tell me what he thinks.

For the Sperlings and the Fishmans
For Andrew and Lilian

Contents

SEVEN BEAUTIES

Something More True Than This   3
Love Poem to the Family   5
Seven Beauties   7
The Dancers   9
Elevator to the Stars   11
Garden   12
Planting   14
Covenant   15
Autobiography   16
Poem to My Brother   17
Specimen   18
Baby-Doll   19
Bar Mitzvah Boy   20
Winter Night   22
When I Left Them   23
My Houdini   24
Closure   25

FLESH AND WORDS

In the meantime,   29
In Kindergarten Class   30
She Masters the Code   31
So Many Grievances   33
Her Imagination Argues Again for the Light of Its Day   34
Light in the Eye   35
Meditation on a Cup of Coffee   36
Making Love   38
Night, Coyote   39
Flesh and Words   42
Study   44
Into   45

DRIVE

Nostalgia   49

Woman Walking Two Dogs   50

When I hear James Dickey   51

Oil   52

Charmer   53

Yawn   54

Credit   55

Genealogy   56

Planter   57

Singing   58

STORM

Husbandry   61

Hearts   62

Tableau with Beautiful Women and Weights   63

An Ocean Between   65

Livno, Bosnia, 1994   67

Bill's Poem   68

Winter Blooms   70

Her Body Wakes Her at 3 a.m.   71

Night Drives in Mating Season   72

Elderly Man Kills Wife, Self   73

Yarn   75

The Unicyclist   77

Andromeda   78

Crimes   79

Test   81

Throwing Wood   82

Equinox   83

Woman in Clay   84

Faith   85

Storm   87

Notes   89

SEVEN BEAUTIES

Something More True Than This

This is how my people ate:
hard-boiled egg in one hand
boiled potato in the other,
a glass of black tea.

Hard-boiled egg in one hand,
I surprise myself some days.
A glass of black tea:
where did I learn to eat this way?

I surprise myself some days
as if from nest to nest, I collect eggs.
Where did I learn to eat this way?
My knuckles red and gnarled

as if from nest to nest, I collect eggs,
as if I earn my bread by my hands,
my knuckles red and gnarled.
When I look in the mirror I see my people.

As if I earn my bread by my hands,
I'm old in their wiry gray hair.
When I look in the mirror I see my people.
Our almond eyes look back darkly.

I'm old in their wiry gray hair.
I don't know my people's names,
our almond eyes look back darkly.
Which streets did we live on?

I don't know my people's names,
and if I go there, to the old country,
which streets did we live on?
What do they need I can give them?

If I go there, to the old country,
boiled potato in my hand,
what do they need I can give them
and how will my people eat?

Love Poem to the Family

I should live so long   The heart holds out
for its miracle.

He should only   His own gall
like a termite
shall eat away at him.

*You should live and be well
a hundred and twenty years.*   More we could not ask for.

More I cannot tell: like stones
better left unturned this *should*
will sometimes appear
as a family trait reappears
years later, on another face—grandmother's wart,
father's wiry Hebrew hair—owned as a hocked jewel
continues to be owned
though it dangles
from a more delicate neck.
A tense unlike past or present,
its speaker would have you believe one foot
is firmly planted in the future.
Olive-skinned and plain, I grew,
and *should* have been
a dutiful daughter.

On Sundays, in Brooklyn,
the extended family gathered
round the ritual deli spread: pastrami,
lean from the bone and riveted
with peppercorns; corned beef;
smoked salmon; whitefish
filleted in its pink hue of fresh meat;

rye sliced thin and hot as the mustard
mingling with faces taking in and issuing out
sounds of chewing, savoring.
And the Yiddish and the English mixed
until meaning emanated from another language—
the children's faces left far behind
in question marks.

Like a secret society
we moved through the bylaws
of cake and coffee, to the final
plum eye in the hysterical
pyramid of apricots guarded by
should live and be well,
against the unknown
but already written.

Seven Beauties

The tall brunettes—
toenails polished a gloss red
to match their lips—
are my mother and her six sisters
in short-shorts: they are the first beauties
I know, *the starlets*
of the bungalow colonies,
those summers of the 1950s.

In pin curls by day, by evening
they let their hair down for dancing,
all *gorgeous* to the owners
and summer staff who milled about
on the outskirts of this wide family circle.
Everyone danced:
on the patio bordering the cement pool,
on the acre of cut grass fanning out
in all directions into the slight breeze
that blew off the Catskills.

The fathers of summer spent their weekdays
at the office, at the store, at the shop
in the steamy city grit.
They traveled home by subway,
railroad, city bus, or cab
to a house on a tree-lined street,
a garden apartment, a triple-decker
where a dog snored welcome.
All summer long the Friday evening highway,
bumper to bumper until the road opened
out to a greener land, trafficked
in husbands bound
to shake two days together
and make of it a summer vacation.

The kids grew—their hair was long,
their hair was short; clothing changed hands.
But the beauties mugging for the camera
were changing imperceptibly through my eyes:
my aunts, before their leap
from black hair to platinum,
and their own cooking caught up with them
at the hips; before their firstborn children
married, had children of their own,
and divorced; before the surprising intimacy
of their marriages became obscured
as a condensing windshield
when vapor and cold glass clash.

My father and six uncles arrived in their blank faces
born of so much absence. They hugged
their tanned wives and kissed their shy
ecstatic children. And the leaving
and the coming together was bitter
and it was sweet, and we were buoyant
until the speedboat that hurtled us
into the next decade jerked,
sputtered, and jerked again.

The Dancers

Long after the Depression receded,
it held with bony fingers

to its place at their table. To say
they were downtrodden was to consider

with singularity one crow from its flock.
He was driven to it secretly at first.

He'd enter the studio as though
he'd shed his skin at the door.

Through the hour, he paid out his dance steps,
each dear coin; his clammy palm

imprinting itself on his partners'
thin waist. But he couldn't keep it

for himself—she was the partner he dreamed,
her slight frame ever so lightly

in his arms. Soon it became their
hidden pleasure. To prepare,

she'd draw the drapes, dim the lights.
He would choose the music

according to the steps he'd learned
the class before: samba, mambo, cha-cha,

waltz; they danced them all in the near dark;
their large and featureless silhouettes

more free, more careless, dipping
and gliding. The shadows danced

and three small children stood the doorway
as if their fantasy world came real,

as if they each were dreaming
the same dream.

Elevator to the Stars

Through her capable hands she lets slide
the elevator's copper gate. Long before she was my mother—
while there were still curls in Shirley Temple's hair—
it was her job to shuttle, as on any ship,
voyagers, up the heavenly shaft
of the Chrysler Building, in the quiet plush
center of its elegance.

In gray gabardine she greets her charges, commends them
to *step to the rear, step lively.*
On a New York day that begins
like any other, there's a commotion, and soon
she's staring into the gay eyes of Bill
"Bojangles" Robinson, his entourage
holding open the doors.

He's making small talk with her, *how goes
the job, what about this heat.* Up through
the single digits and on
to the double, she's in his light—talking,
mincing with Bojangles and already
another, past tense voice takes it home,
shapes the story. At seventy-eight,

all it takes is a broad-brimmed sombrero,
black and exotic atop my mother's silver head
to restore glamour to its pedestal. The word *allure*
straightens its seams, fascination recovers its thrill.
I see now my enchantment is in the silk lining of her presence
how she carries her past in the folds
of her raiment, the attitude of a hat.

Garden

In rich soil under
the tall pine in front of my parents' red
brick house, my mother half planted:
spatulas, butter knives, soup ladles;
all the luckless utensils of her orthodoxy.

Not the happy spoon of the rhyme
who ran away with the dish,
her patterned stainless fell
folly to our forgetfulness. We knew
meat and milk don't mix,
but between the knowing
and the doing an innocent spoon
was banished to dirt
until harvest. Burdened by a role
in religious life, two separate
armies of kitchenware lined
the shelves and drawers on opposite
sides of the sink.

                    Why is it,
my friends would ask, *your mother*
plants her silver? This question
sat long among the odd behaviors
that bloomed like cutlery in our garden:
the Sabbath darkness we groped in
rather than affront God with electric
light, the bacon
we shunned, the stuffed derma
we savored, the menorah in the window
at Christmas.

Venerable roots ground such faith
in this plant that does not bend.
The heavens and I as witness, my mother
upside-down interred those shafts:
serrated, pronged, and bowled,
exhausted her shame of us in earth.

Planting

God knows what obstacles protrude from the earth
between me and a flower bed that thrives.

As though it were not enough to dig
their doom myself, my mother stands over me

meting out spade, seedling, watering can,
advising as only a New York City gardener will.

In their thin plastic containers perennials
promise blue, purple, salmon:

a proliferation of blooms
rivaled only by that first garden; a link

to knowledge they might still
interpret had it not been bred out of them.

And as an optimist without a shred
of evidence, she can tell you you are never

turned away at the nursery door, no matter
how many delphiniums, columbines, or *allium giganteum*

have fallen to your thumb.
In this way, we are always preparing,

my mother and I, a bed for accomplishment;
practicing pride for what might grow;

planting seeds of agreement—
something green and admirable that could greet her

next summer, or the next, or the one after that,
in a riot of clashing color.

Covenant

The child I might have been stands on the threshold
of her father's bedroom, lit with curiosity
at the breathy wonder of this body,
rhapsodic in a murmuring conversation
with God.

A formal man winding phylacteries in morning prayer,
he rocks himself in a constant bow. What do I know?
I throw open the door to be taken up
into the arms of this half-sung dialogue
between father and the invisible receiver of low tones.

At his bedside we are clefts
drawn through the staff the Venetian blind casts,
and the white light matches the black bands
I can't take my eyes from: one wound
up my father's arm, the other bound to his forehead.

In a further covenant, my father places an assurance
on top of my head—ask no questions daughter.
It is his wide heavy palm that lingers. a skullcap
I might have worn under a cloud
protecting the sky from my blasphemy.

Autobiography

When I write my autobiography
I do not mention you.

In my recreated childhood
there is no menace

on this side of my door.
Nothing jumps me

from behind. No one
punches my small arms sore.

I struggle the words
up from the depths where as children

ours were banished. There your voice
is still. When I cry

it is not so bitter a taste
that I am alien

even to my own sorrow.

Poem to My Brother

In a circus family everyone specializes.
You perfected the disappearing:

each stunt taking you farther away,
until, in one spectacular moment, you vanished.

It's fourteen years later and why you left
is still the mystery I try to crack. Today,

I'm a tall woman with a teenaged daughter.
A few of the rest are still here

in their poses, makeup a little sloppy now.
Such a large tribe back then, such an unruly family.

I remember as kids we swore we'd never
not talk to each other like some of Mom's sisters.

If we'd been rich, oh, if only we'd been rich,
everything and nothing would've been different.

I know there were days under the big top:
comic book and canned soup days;

days we resembled each other—same awkward mouth
twisted in not a kind smile, same darkness under

already dark skin. What I mean is,
we were just kids in the kitchen

having what I thought was the same childhood.
But it's never the same.

Nothing held us up and there was no net
to catch us as we fell.

Specimen

Bug boy, my nemesis, is on the loose.
Glass jar and lid in hand, he terrorizes all of us
in the insect world.

He's after my invisible wings,
their iridescent greens and yellows: kid sister,
monarch butterfly, common lazy housefly,
prized praying mantis. We're all flying recklessly

around and around to save ourselves,
and our coded sounds overlap so none of us feel his hot
harried breath on our small bodies.

Along one wall of his bedroom, straight pins
still the lives of his prey. I understand
with every throb of my punched-up arms.

He's a hitter, my brother David, King of Threats
and I never bow down low enough to salute him,
never tie myself in enough knots to entertain him,
never convey the right amount of reverence to honor him.

Why's he so mad?
Why are his blows forgiven boy's play?
Why is his maleness gold in the family currency?

Run little girl, he's right behind you, run.
I want to reach my huge arm into the past,
scoop her out of danger.

I want to spill him from the jar moments before the mad
adolescent scientist impales him to the wall
with all his speared insect companions,
their once powerful stingers shriveled,
so many hushed bugs.

Baby-Doll

You were the boy with the paper route
instructing me in the all important fold.

Who knew what you looked like
balancing the bike

and your enormous load?
We never followed to cheer you on,

snap you
for the family album.

Older brother to a girl
whose call was to play at house,

what could have seemed more
superfluous to a boy painter,

boy scientist? But when the contest
was announced something drove you

to sell the most subscriptions.
What the other prizes were

I never knew. The baby-doll,
in her new plastic smell,

you placed in my arms.

Bar Mitzvah Boy

Announced into Jewish society, you rocked and rolled
across the ballroom floor. Do I remember it right?
The overlit room of chandelier brightness, mirrors
reflecting back at us multiple images of you.
Dazzles of women in sweeping gowns, freshly minted
young girls at the dais rustling their pre-prom regalia:

excesses earmarked for your coming out.
Wedding of the boy—boy still in shape and size—
to his newly turned-out manhood.
You were an unlikely prince
in your tux; your brilliantined hair—the duck's ass,
we teased—curling forward into your eyes.

But the role had been laid out for you
like your clothes that morning,
born to it, no kicking and screaming
to the bima. Celebrated
at thirteen by virtue of your gender, your family
in all its extended largesse stood applauding

as at the opera for the tenor who
steps out alone before his adoring fans
to accept what he has earned. You sang—
a little nasal—the memorized text
in Hebrew without ever having understood
what the symbols meant. Did you love

the attention? Did you believe God's staff
was yours? Who knows what you believed.
Mornings, your father bends in silent devotion
to God, *Blessed art thou, Lord our God,* he praises,
King of the Universe, who has not made me a woman.
Twice blessed, and thankful. For what are you thankful?

For the satellites we made of ourselves illuminating
your path to clear center? For the overflowing cup
of unwavering faith you had but to drink from?
For a family, teeming with aging attendants and ladies
in waiting—and having left us all
grinning in our places?

Winter Night

To this fourteen-year-old, everything about a winter night is provocative: the way the snow keeps on in purple hues even after the two of them face off; the way my brother's face contorts with wordlessness; and my mother's animated face swoops in close to his as if to lick away tears. I don't know why this awful exchange is taking place out there in the snow. I can't hear them two stories up in the overheated apartment. In my fear of him, I think it must have something to do with me. What have I done? He's four years older than I am, tall and strong; what could I do to him? In my fear of her, I think when she returns she'll turn a different face on me. He's jacketless; she's coatless, in her slippers. I know she roams the neighborhood because she's gone a long while. She doesn't know where he might go. She doesn't know his friends; none of us know them. She doesn't know him; none of us know him. The more she realizes this, the more frightened she becomes. The more I realize this, as I stand at the window, the deeper I bite into my cuticles. I draw blood as if the red sting will mean something against what I imagine is to come. I imagine through that door the outside will come in, and I will never be warm again. Much later, the two of them round the corner, her arm draped over my brother; defeat, exhaustion, and the winter night allow this closeness, which will dissolve inside the threshold. I want the two of them to continue to arrive, and never enter. If they could forever arrive, I could stand here. When my blood dries, I could bite again, deep into the wound. This is the bargain I make with God, to keep them outside, to keep them together.

When I Left Them

The day was ordinary.
It was drawn up from the stifling sameness
of years of days that now jelled brilliantly
into one insect wing
I would flick off.
I was suspended
in a heightened state of last acts,
conveyed from bed
along the belt of little civilities
for my teeth, my bowels,
my whole ecstatic body.

Rooms I walked in and out of
shrank and closed up behind me.
There was that last look into their faces;
I expected to wince.
I scraped out of myself those other selves: son, brother,
husband, and father.
I bounded out of that skin,
past all the arms that held me,
through shouts of disassociated words: sounds
belonging to a woman, her children,
a barking dog.

My Houdini

Not like Tony Curtis in the movie version of Houdini's life,
my Houdini disappeared. And every day since he left,
his mother waits for a sign.

Under the ice continent, in his blue hue
of panic, the real Houdini searched the ice mass
for the opening his faith assured him was there.

Frozen as a beetle in amber
the past slowed my brother until he disengaged its heavy shell,
breathed water and swam through.

His mother heard the drip she hoped
was polar ice melting and flushing
down the earth's crevasse.

She heard her own doubt loosen its cap
and unleash the accumulated steam
of his desire to leave her.

My Houdini's kinky hair
never loses its shape, never snakes round
his brilliant face.

In bedroom blue water, he swims toward me; we lock arms.
Having hold of him, as if we'd been Siamese twins,
the half-store of our split selves comes whole.

In the Hollywood ending, I'm the selfless deliverer
who restores the hero to his family.
He is the trophy I struggle along with to the surface.

Closure

I wish to speak boldly finally
in the exclusive tongue of past tense:
yes, I would say, *he died; it was a long and terrible ordeal,*
it was.

What I want, while I'm handling it, is to know
this is the last infested log of blame
I'll throw on that fire;
what's left is only ash.

Even the deadbolt
rides friction through its cylinder
and has, in the end, a long, satisfying
glide-click into place.

What I have heaves: a rib cage
that rattles, and rises and falls.
In my dreams of him, my brother is vengeful or loving, and I worry
we'll come to know even Limbo as a better place
than this place.

FLESH AND WORDS

In the meantime,

I recommend *Moby Dick*
to mothers and fathers about to be launched.
Champagne to the hull:
it's Ahab this, and Queequeg that;

boats, water, whales.
Through bathed ears the fetus hears
the intonation of drama,
drama of action, action's expectations—oh

expectations—we each harbored a craft
fully furnished with unraveling dreams;
each of us dreaming in the red glow
that penetrates the membrane of sleep.

What became of sleep?
My dull body stretched the length
of the unborn one's numbered days,
until the bow of the boat split

up the middle from a whiteness so grave,
I peed into my socks
and opened my fists
to greet my flesh.

In Kindergarten Class

How quickly the small plastic chair
diminishes me.
Facing me in an identical
blue shrunken chair is my daughter's teacher.
I hear myself confess to inadequacies
that bang around down the chamber
of my origins, and the shine
of embarrassment is on me.
My arms fly in these confidences,
my wild face dances.
I know she can absolve me,
or that she might with eraser and chalk
correct and rechart
a six-year-old's course
in the world without me.

She Masters the Code

Through trust
and the repetition of sounds:
A E I O U, the world moves
and she does, closer
to the word.
In her need to glide
on the under-
surfaces, to trace her figures
in ever-expanding shapes,
how chameleonlike
words seem to her—
given the company
they keep.
At seven, just as her hands
mime a more delicate movement,
and her legs propel her
straight to the mark,
her mind enters a field
where each revelation uncovers
something overlapped: a fish
inside a larger fish.
We spell out loud,
and I celebrate the little-
heralded passage of the child-
turned-reader. She plunges
into variety and texture
as if she is an entirely
new species: one
who breathes in the layers
between what is said
and what is meant. Now,
when she asks me why,
my daughter's eyes

let me know
she requires the long
explanation
that takes us
into the greedy realm
of her new appetite.

So Many Grievances

When I was a child it was exasperation
from being named last that held me
in the pivot of my step.
My mother would stammer across
the stream of names that swam up
in her *need-to-be-in-charge* voice.

In that longest moment
we'd stare at each other
from opposite sides of her distraction.
She'd sing out Ilene, Sondra, Dinah,
blowsy first cousins whose ready names arrived
long before she ever got to mine.

I called my daughter a name
when her father placed her wriggling body,
cheesy with the newness of her life,
on my belly. I called it
without looking into his eyes
for agreement.

I called it out
in celebration of her face
turning from purple-blue to pink
before my eyes.
In my child's sixth year,
what I want to say to my mother,

past my daughter's disbelief at me
as I sort wildly among family names
arrowing through time and space
to pin my voice on hers, is:
so many of my grievances
are undone.

Her Imagination Argues Again
for the Light of Its Day

My daughter hears voices. They are the random voices of a crowd:
some complain, some philosophize, but one is overly anxious to be heard:
it has her attention. To listen, she stills her ready hand,

rubs her charcoal-smeared face. For her,
it is a diving board, this precipice.
This girl comes to it with determination and grace

knowing she must train the line of her body,
tuck of her head. From the precise slice of water
she begins her journey to air.

The line Lilian is compelled to draw in charcoal, over and over,
has something to do with this. Around her body accidental shapes
are everywhere. She trains her eyes

to this way of seeing. This way of seeing the absence of line
makes line possible. The teacher insists, *curve your hand
this way, shade the area as I do,* but she cannot.

She is electric, lit with anger
and brings her hand through a black sweep
across the paper.

The fact of the line brings not silence, but a hum
to her thoughts as they fall together. Images fly
behind her eyes faster than she can convey them

to paper. Lines converge, continue off the page: her wrist,
her arm, her body; she steps away, becomes a new shape,
an end and a beginning.

Light in the Eye

If these fit you,
        I tell her
they're yours and remember my mother
        about to wriggle her ring guard off
from its long-standing, protective place
        beside her wedding band.

I have many things
        I've hoarded
over half a lifetime, and never meant
        to relinquish.

A giddy letting go
        presses me now
into its service.

I pile her outstretched arms
        with folded clothes
no longer dress-up:
        purples and blues,
wools and corduroys;
        her eyes lit with it;
eyes, which I saw, followed the route
        of her bounty.

I'm not changed,
        though to see her now—young *Helen,*
bright one—in my clothes,
        we are.

Meditation on a Cup of Coffee

The secret of her mother's perked coffee
was a little salt in the grounds.

In the aluminum pot, boiled water bubbled up
through the basket. Outside the family,

only an old boyfriend knew.
The glass thimble that topped the lid

popped with the sound
of the dark liquid

as it washed
up and down.

The coffee's aroma traveled, in its cartoonlike
trail, through the rooms.

She can see the figure of a woman: dark coat,
pocketbook fixed to an arm, as she jabs

around the narrow kitchen, procuring the pot
from a low cupboard, grounds from the freezer.

She tried them all: the large shapely hourglass
with the filter and grounds in the top,

the glass pot with the removable funnel,
the European model with the infuser

that shimmies down inside the length
of the slim glass vial. Always the glass slipped

from her hands and shattered into slivers
or tapped against the faucet and separated

into two perfectly useless pieces of glass.
All the while the tap runs, her coat puffs out,

she's picking up speed, desperate for it now.
The girl in the doorway observes.

Her mother makes a pot of coffee. It's late
and she's just returned home from work.

Recalling this nightly ritual,
and the singularity of the figure

in her memory,
she thinks again of selfishness, and knows

the aroma of this word to be rich
and good as brewed coffee.

Making Love

They compare everything to the past:
the coarse gray hair, the extra roll

of flesh, the aches and pains
no longer imagined.

Let's go to bed, she said.
Too early, he said.

I need to lie in your arms, she said.
The thin top sheet was cover enough.

She pulled it over his sharp shoulder blades
anticipating his chill. Body heat

rose and spread until heat, flesh, sheet, bed,
room, house, circled out and away from them.

Their sounds drowned out all others, but
there were crickets below the open windows, bird song

in the trees, and squirrel chatter. There was daylight
and there were summer temperatures.

There were the two of them
and they had been talking.

There was the past, the hulk of its shadow
still visible.

And there was more that they could not see
coming from a great distance.

Night, Coyote

1

Past the kept lawn, a pack of coyotes
assembles. Their song
is a charm to a pair of lovers.

Through flung-open windows,
a breeze blows over them.
They're grateful

their lovemaking was long
and tightened the drum
of their bodies.

2

He tells her he's happy.
Daytime is the time
for such happiness, she knows.

At night the papery walls of happiness dissolve
in the coyote's watery laughter
that comes after their song.

3

In bed she rolls toward his fiery body
that trembles in his deep hell
of happiness.

She doesn't know her sleeping husband.
His night-self pitches and shakes.
She fears for her own sleep.

4

These same dense trees, forty feet straight up,
don't sway, don't wave their pine fingers
in the moonlessness.

The night-rigid bodies close in.
When you wake in this dream of waking
you're surrounded, a babe among beasts.

Their thorn tongues work you over
until your skin glistens, until finally
your body tumbles out of the dream.

5

Last night they were closer than they've ever been.
Their voices climbed high enough to cross the yard.
Neither in the bedroom said

did you hear or *they're so close*;
the atmospheres of sleep and waking
thoroughly mingled.

6

The farmer down the road calls them
coy-dogs; refuses to allow
that the pure breed traveled

so far to find itself
in a country of chickens
and kitchen gardens.

7

The well-built house, with its deep separation,
inside from out, is an illusion
of protection.

She bends to sort glossy paper from news,
remembers the long night past;
his tortured sleep keeping her

from her own.
In the yard and beyond
nothing visible moves.

Flesh and Words

1

Back when we believed everything
our hands and tongues taught us,
intimacy was easy.

I should have plucked the lyre
then, should have memorialized for all time
the magnificent kiss,

prelude to acts I took for granted
the body was created to commit.
A woman I didn't know warned me

in her desperate, aged voice *love
your estrogen* and I, though ignorant
and young, turned it

over and over as layer
after layer fell away
and revealed itself to me.

2

The sixteen-year-old is irreverent and mocking
about menopause; she can afford it.
I listen to her yodel

as if from a mountaintop to a valley.
In middle age so many women I know
still whisper the word—

all that's missing is a secret handshake
below each grimace. The words
still haven't dried on the flyers

after all these centuries of women growing old.
The change, my own mother's favorite euphemism,
haunts with its own accompaniment of eerie echoes.

It's no wonder gynecologists
and TV advertisers are the only ones
talking out loud about the physics

of my body: a not altogether sad story
for generations of women
whose bodies we know

transform on the inside while with chisel
and hammer, we hew a rough thing,
as from rock, to speak of it.

Study

I'm a liar nights looking up at you
from my squinty glance into the lens: yes,
I see three stars form an arrow;

yes to the Archer, Canis Major,
likewise Minor. There is no science
similar to how I study you.

Board by board, I watched you bang nails,
deck this platform—
your paean to the stars.

Tonight, the double-star
half-hiding her mate, orbits a path
invisible to your eye. The telescope

tipped up on its stand extends your whole body
where you'd willingly go
into the unknowable.

You run the gravel track
to exhaust yourself, push your body to pain
as if it won't find its own way.

I know what you suffer is more than curiosity
and so I'm grateful for gravity
which holds you here.

Into

In fall
as bulbs go down
the chutes of a long
winter, chain saws sputter
their crude recommendation
for a small fire, and we face each other
as if to scrutinize the landscape
of our contentedness.
Inventorying along the beaten lines
of skin: November, December, the hairpin turn
into January, and still the frigid months
peel on the dry air.

Now gossip stops
to dance out the cold news
of other couples failing
the surprise quiz. I look into your bloodshot eyes
to recognize, not a haven keeping me glazed
with fire above the towering out-of-doors,
but a storm-cellar entry into
a quiet humor, making of weather
a piled-high, frozen toboggan slide
out on our backs
into spring.

DRIVE

Nostalgia

To hear what I'm thinking,
I have to get back in the car,
for others it's books on tape.
In a new basic '76 mustard-colored Toyota,
sans radio for six hours
I drove and sang
every song I knew in my life.
I didn't repeat one.
That was a great car.

Woman Walking Two Dogs

I saw her but I didn't really,
you know what I mean.
I could tell you her hair
was strawberry blonde
and smelled of thousands
of generous brush strokes and
what my hands felt cradled in it.
I wasn't even driving fast.
The dogs pulled in different directions,
then she turned away.

When I hear James Dickey

say "Cherrylog Road" (on the LP), I admit
I want to be his Doris Holbrook. It's the combination
of passion and ingenuity I admire.
She's a woman who knows what to do
with her lips and a wrench.
In the wildness of the moment,
Dickey catches me up. It's the heat,
the springs in her back, the eye of the animal on her
and, to get what she needs,
Doris's willing drive between lust and fear.

Oil

The stick is dry. I do believe in,
yet overlooked, this omen.
We're driving and talking:
conversations in cracked voices
sputter, jerk, halt. We might as well be
sitting in a darkened theater facing a screen
where all the real drama is
safely contained. The unpredictable husband
is agitated, his wife
may be mad.

Charmer

On a drive through farm country,
one car's behind me for miles.
As we kick dust, his mouth moves
in my rearview mirror, his eyelids aflutter.
I see a microphone gripped in his hand,
and a pomade gleam in his hair.
I smell the cigarette cloud he's in
and I want a drag off that ecstasy.
I'm searching for little Havana
on the car radio and singing
the cows all the way home.

Yawn

I love the woman who yawns,
arms swinging, full-face
unabashedly into the day.
Through a car window, I love
to see part of what makes us
human. Her yawn begets
my yawn, and my hands
never leave the wheel.

Credit

My gas card is a relative to the new
hotel key: made of flat plastic
embedded with intelligence,
some slide through a magnetic groove,
some sit briefly in a metal pocket
on a door. There are probably others
that then swing open another world
where you can be someone
who needs a wake-up call,
flips the "do not disturb" sign.

Genealogy

My eyes scan beyond the car's inconstant horizon.
Time and time again, they pass
over, perched atop the wheel, my hands.
Of course I see my mother's hands there;
and it's the others' hands there
I see. Laborers all, scattered over Europe,
I don't know which little towns were home
to them. How easy with a map and names,
to point the car in that direction
and go.

Planter

Up to its windows in mean weeds
out the back door, it wasn't an imposition
so much as it was wrong: a car so long
immobile, stripped of its dignity. It still
went, but it wouldn't take us
into the nineties in the style
we believed we deserved.

Singing

Where am I free?
I'm on my way. I don't know where
I'm going.
In the car,
I come closest to the flying I did
on my mattress
with its exuberant lift-off,
the windows open out sideways
and I'm off.

STORM

Husbandry

Forsaken, one hand taps the damp wicker
while one Adam's son invents a running game down one ark length
and up the other. Another

tutors animals in conversation,
in song, to dance a two-step. Marble, wand of coal, divination:
the same old story.

Humans try on monkey habits, dog and hyena;
cross-legged on the wide wooden floorboards,
we examine the hairs on our arms,

worry our splinters,
trim each other's toenails, conduct a symphony of animal exhalations;
leery animals look away.

God, it's all weather here!
Every soul complains of every sense assailed.
What we couldn't do with a little dry land.

What's a shark's tooth of doubt
in the face of faith? Rubbery legs will carry us down
the wobbly planks;

some of us, I know,
will take to all fours.
It's a piddling light when at last it comes.

Hearts

Hearts have not been broken
the leisurely pronouncement is made
long after barbecue, and the kids' one last swim
hot into the night
of cards.

I can't see it any other way:
the black queen mocks me from my hand.
I tell you they have.
These shards of black and red
fall to the wiped clean table and I mistake them,

not for a game, but pictures from my life,
or the tarot, left face up for all to see.
Four women I love, each in a suit,
each house threatened with toppling.
Another set of losses,

pass off to the right
what we can't afford to be left with.
This orderly world within my waking world,
I shuffle, arrange, discard,
and play a new hand.

Novice at the table,
I can't grasp the game.
All the while, one who plays to win
hoards cards—hearts all—
shoot the moon.

Tableau with Beautiful
Women and Weights

Some of us work weights to secure
what might be fallen,
for others it's a respite from despair.

We notice the durable body
that's been there all along, trusty
as a bicycle. We turn to it,

our mode of transport to the interior.
There is pain we give ourselves over to
willingly and can't imagine afterwards

our gratitude. These deep stretches
are a journey then along the inner flanks
aboard a minuscule ship,

a fantastic voyage
coursing through blood.
Every tendon, sinew, ligament,

and the skin aligns its movement
with the rhythm of the heart
and every next note pumps up

to a sharper, more acute pain. My friend
paces the sidelines, her steady breath
and the musical beat overtaken

by an inner insistent voice that conspires
against the organization of her thoughts.
The easy word between us flutters away.

How can the brain and its body
wage such war?
Later, she bends to caress

her hard-working legs, to soothe them
through a transparency she can reach
to pain she can touch.

I loiter just beyond the gates
of her despair. My friend and I meet there
several times a week where

stretched to trembling,
there is such forgiveness
in our bodies.

An Ocean Between

Valentina is home for the summer
in Karelia's green afternoon dreaming
in Russian again, the table set

with sour cream and borscht in brown crockery,
an alphabet of familiar sounds crooning
to her and her American-born daughter.

Their shapes march then float up easy
as Russian thoughts but an ocean boils
between the shores of mother tongue

and a language whose heart she hasn't yet found.
In the yard of the house where she was raised
generations line up, mingle; an arbor opens

where grapes hang low or is it just the romantic in me
remembering what I cannot know. Heaven over Russia
is more than stars in a dark sky.

Only once my grandmother crossed that ocean
over which my friend flies.
It's what is mirrored there

in the faces of her sisters, her babushka—
mine fled pogroms, poverty, a husband
and two sons—they were black spots

on her old heart—though I'll never know why.
I taught her *see Spot run* from my primer,
but English never took. That family is lost

to me even if I could find the ones who live. Now
Valentina reaches the shore and breaks
her own trail, drives her memories

deep into a foreign country, through Russian thoughts
that battle their way to English
and the slow furl of her tongue.

Livno, Bosnia, 1994

In the smallest U.S. capital, I meet a young mother
learning to speak English. Opened before us a book
of color photographs and on the page,

moist plums. She tells me she grew fruit trees—
not a few in a garden—but row upon fragrant row,
clear to the horizon.

Thirty years ago, I want to tell her, a farmer bored with potatoes
planted thousands of saplings on his open fields. I live there
with my family under the swaying tops

of forty-foot Norway pines. We could draw a straight line we could not
follow from this New England town to that abandoned orchard
in Livno. Neither planter nor pruner,

I imagine those trees burdened without her, ripe plums
and the ground mottled with rotting fruit,
black with bones.

Bill's Poem

I'm all over town looking for cannoli
for my friend Bill: cracked ribs and leg fractures
laid up in a hospital far from home

for walking at night on a road
between lampposts, snow banked so high
the sidewalk is an unreachable parallel

where he's walked before in spring and fall and returned
body and soul intact. Earlier in the day,
the conversation turned to cannoli

filled with chocolate for a twist
and we're tasting it. Then, last night,
he's picked off by a speeding teen

with better than the legal limit of drink in him.
I start out looking in the logical places
where seductions of fresh pastries tease

behind low glass counters.
None is cannoli
and Bill would know being from the Bronx.

I hurry and end up in a Gas/Mart
whose sandwiches, salads, cakes and pastries, creaseless
in Saran, stiffen beyond their expiration dates.

I'm hoping for cannoli—
even a trophy replica—so at very least Bill's eyes
see something, besides himself, out of place

in a hospital room. Meds are warring
in his body. He's not eating, or sitting up,
or moving around. There's not enough oxygen

in his lungs. *I'm an ox*, he says, Bill
who never gets sick, never broke a bone.
Two days later, in a private room, he says,

I'm thinking maybe I shouldn't walk on the road at night any more.
I'm thinking maybe I shouldn't come to Vermont any more.
Before my eyes the world begins to shrink.

No, I tell him, *that's not living.*
Then I reprise the cannoli
how there isn't one to be had

in this town, chocolate or otherwise,
and I see his mouth open to it
ever so slightly.

Winter Blooms

Forcing is a deception;
these buds come willingly.
River stones and water,

six paper whites in a blue bowl.
A store of bulbs in paper bags
in the icebox. Darkness and cold saving

those onion skins for successive winter blooms.
Successive implies patience, a period of waiting,
like pregnancy. The first narcissus withers

as light snow powders the outside beds.
The perennial bed harbors the bearded iris,
the one-day lily. *Successive* implies restraint.

I pot every bulb until crockery covers
the interior landscape. All the chilly bulbs
stationed in the stones, the cold white stones

gleam in water, pull down
the tendril roots. Spring green
shoots cross and lean; winter

is at the window, having its way,
forcing. An army of paper whites
holds it at bay.

This is the place to be, to wait it out,
rolled tight and dormant, a stone
in a burgeoning bed.

Her Body Wakes Her at 3 a.m.

On her back under a moist sheet
she feels the beginning of a pain
in her breast—that exotic fruit
erect under the cover.

The pain is small, she tells herself,
smaller than the night will allow.
The throb separates her from the rest
of herself. It hovers

as a portrait of her mother might,
hung over her bed, hands
still as flesh on a battlefield.
She shivers down the length

of her body—skimpy body
she dragged along
the sickly green halls of junior
high school,

bumped on all sides by girls with breasts,
breasts that arrived in seventh grade
as part of the new curriculum. Hormones
careened through their bodies,

sharpened teenage cruelty. Then the boys
singled out her flat chest, their graffiti
covered the green blackboards with testimonials
to her shortcomings.

Ech, she scrapes the sound
from the back of her throat, the irony
of so small a detail clamoring
for her attention now.

Night Drives in Mating Season

The longer I don't encounter him
the deeper my conviction
we'll meet on that winding road between the diamond

signs—MOOSE—on a ten-mile stretch
of blacktop cut through green mountains.
Curves in the road, low shoulders, moose like

to linger. Deer in the headlights freeze then
scatter; they've had their eulogies. At night,
mine is the only light, a heart-shaped beacon

for a ton of moose. I imagine it slow as ballet:
the impact propels the body
through the windshield. I alternate

between speeding through the night, to make it home
before my wavering eyes shut finally, and creeping
along in anticipation of the bull moose who, monolithic, waits

in the middle of the road, another dimension of darkness
to cradle us both. Everyone I know
who's seen one relishes his moose-sighting story.

But he's not the one who saw it up close
and didn't live to tell. I'm staring down the dark body
of a moose in the middle of the night

and this much is clear: this is an intersection
with no signs to divine
if I'm awake or this is a dream.

When I reach my destination, I wonder
how I got there, a whipped-up landscape
unraveled behind me.

Elderly Man Kills Wife, Self

When he looked deep into himself
as he must have to take it on,
into the familiar pool
where as a boy he swam alone,
he saw how no configuration of ledge
could snag him, no fierce hole
could entice him to continue down,
down where he was without her.

She was there wherever he saw himself.
He believed her to be the voice answering
outside his hearing all those years
of not knowing himself. Her body
and the memory of her body all day long
gave substance and weight to his own
reedy, colorless body,
which he needed
and which she in her ease without words
taught him in signs her eyes, hands,
shoulders, and legs made fluently.

She was a moon circling; it suited her
if he fancied himself the center.
For his part, what was familiar and constant
was simple, he didn't question how he came to be
this man. Suddenly alone,
the finality of rooms, untouched
since he'd driven her that morning,
would be snapshots he'd carry in his mind.
The plan fell into place then as if it had always been there,
a destination they had been traveling toward without
acknowledgment, though not unknowingly.
The hospital had already drained
what strength she had left. She was beyond

her own recognition and listened to him
tell her everything at once, the sweet
mundane horrors of what he'd eaten
rather than cook, mixed in a crazy jumble
with wanting her and their life,
what having neither had done to him.

That was when he read her the note,
a simple statement of fact,
We decided we don't want anymore,
and brought the gun softly to her.
She understood he was too much with wanting,
and that her wait for him would not be long.

Yarn

He watches her
out of the corner of his eye
seated next to him in the Greyhound,
she the aisle, he the window.

He wears a gray suit, briefcase
on his lap and in his hands
the *Times* folded, and folded again,
which is called for in tight spaces,
but he's not reading.

Her long blond hair shines.
Her fingers fly, caught
between yarn and the silver hook
in a rhythm that draws him
little by little into her light
until his head turns
and then his body
and if he'd been her lover
he'd be that close.

He has to say something
or this intimacy he's created
will turn itself loose
and that is not his destination.

He's a businessman,
she's a college student crocheting
something purple
though he doesn't know it to be
crocheting; he'd have called it knitting.
She is all smiles at his interest,
which she might assume is in her
and in part it may be, but it's also
something else.

He is a man in a gray suit
on a bus on a highway
and in this moment away from all
that's familiar, away from anyone
who could call him by name,
he could be anyone.
He could be a man who knows
the feel of purple yarn wound
round his thumb and forefinger
working the silver hook methodically,
slowly in and out, easy and loose.
He sees himself as that man;
he is that man.

The Unicyclist

My son pedals a unicycle;
pedal is all my son does.
I shout at him; it is his pleasure
that concerns him.

In the street I juggle groceries.
Slush hurls itself at me.
Through the crack between the bags
I see one thin wheel.

I shout at him in my head,
my son, with his insufferable balance,
whose free hand feeds cigarettes
to the raw circle of his mouth.

In my head I hear what he thinks of me,
the dumpy mother who held him back
from his first steps.
I smack him when he least expects

contact, touch. The smack
is in my head now. I was young
and he was nothing. It was my choice.

Andromeda

Twice the kids circle the cliff edge
on their banana-seated racers.
For a long time they ogle something
noisy through the bushes.
Sighs, gargled laughter, and splashing water:
a fat naked woman heaving such waves,
a whale in the lake
wouldn't have surprised them.

Between the branches, they see
her breasts float, pink and buoyant;
dragonflies skim the darker surface.
She flaps and dives and pulls her feet in
to follow. Through the tangled roots
they converge on her.

Switches raised, they poke
the brush in small taunting
jabs. From the water she hears
rustling and stops herself.
Muscles stiffen, a cramp
curls her foot in on itself.
Eyes are on her,
she shivers the water.

Crime

1

The woman on the evening news stares at her upturned palms. She says she is *sorry for the families of the dead men*. She doesn't say a small green worm pokes its head out of the hole in her hand or that her heart floods her body continuously with blood so thick she knows it will smother her. She doesn't speak again because the only true words, she believes, would have to travel from very far away, from a volume of truth in which her name and the name of her son, who pulled the trigger, are written together, one superscripted, the other, hers, exalted from the moment of his birth.

2

I haven't written you this week while you've been at summer camp. Your sad letters say you miss me, you love me. I mistrust your homesick declarations, your fourteen-year-old shot in the darkness lit by a dim flashlight. I mistrust what I would write—words transforming my misshapen heart caught in the torque of our bodies separating, which I know must be, and which I see must wrench.

What I see written on your face when you look at me sometimes is all the heartlessness you turn on what you despise. You don't see me. Maybe you can't. Maybe that sightlessness is a condition of youth meant to protect those abandoned on the street. You turn it on me sure as a loaded gun. I turned it on my own mother, each killing look eroding love. *Do you think I don't feel?*

It won't always be this way, the mothers tell me. He'll change again and again, and someday you'll be talking together, and all the old hurt will fall away. I can't hear them, the mothers of grown children. They've already forgotten the breathtaking purity of what the child knows. They've forgotten this, as I've forgotten the pain of your birth; such forgetting is paramount if the species is to continue.

3

The woman on the TV news hesitates to think she is a mother. The chasm she must cross to remember this is perilous. To protect herself she stands only on its brink, every muscle in her body tight, her eyes squinting to shut out a too-bright light. The woman knows what she knows in her blood, the way she knows to avert her eyes from the eyes of the female reporter when she asks why would the woman's son do this thing; what would be his motivation? As if surely she knows.

Test

Autumn is a test of the true blue
who labor out of season

in the perennial bed. Between the withered cosmos
and the unwound trumpet flower,

I find my ready faith in plants I know will return
and follow as it thins along its tenuous byways to what cannot be

touched, known. I haven't always believed the neat green leaves,
haven't ever called it God's work. Long after I plant the bulbs,

I switch from hand spade to bare fingers and dig deep
in the cold earth. There I plant my vivid desire both scented

and radiant. Before the sun flashes out
into its winter pale, its heat I pack down hard

and hold my hands on the mound
of what faith I bury.

Throwing Wood

Littered with bark and flecks of wood,
the cord rows stacked long and low by March
dry and decompose until log by log
we haul them out of the woodshed below.

From above, I watch myself descend
the rickety ladder in man-sized clothes
protecting me from the harm of dead wood.
The wood cellar is a room contained
in its own nature, wood dust settled,
already muffling the sounds I bring
with my bulk.

Over the tops of log rows I roll my soles,
hoist split wood from here to there
and once again through the trap
to be stacked in the shed above.

Below, in the great escape
of wood-throwing, my senses rule
without instruction. In the lively silence
between eyes and hands,
wood slips through my grasp.

The body's language is one I speak
as a cave woman. Then thighs
and arms and back recall
the birth muscle tightening, burning,
and letting go. There in the blast cold
wood cellar, I remember giving birth
to fire.

Equinox

Facts are scattered everywhere
as the snow melts, and the ground
is uglier than I remember.

What I mean is, I'm a seasonal person
halted, while emergence tugs
at all the tender hearts around me.

I know it's true,
I can swallow myself.
But what if I had only this day

for discovery? I want to dance too,
instead of watching
like an insect turned on its back

as I, upside-down, spin a little.

Woman in Clay

Last night in the clay on my slab
I saw a woman whose head
and face were born into my palms,
damp and furrowed with the effort.

Enormous shoulders—broad in anticipation
of what she would hoist upon herself—
broke free. Her breasts
and belly undulated

with the roll of my fingers.
The more I stroked,
the sharper her features appeared.
Her scalp I striated

and wetted with slip
so the hair would adhere.
I gave her strings of clay wrung
through a garlic press;

it flew in all directions,
a crazy headdress for the occasion.
At last, I reached up my hand inside her,
and delivered us each from the other.

Faith

The black beans soak. To put them up
   an act of pure optimism. Tomorrow, the cast-iron kettle
      will simmer black water, will foam blue-black, but for tonight

these closed jewels are a bridge to whatever rises with the light.
   I'm not saying I'll sleep easier, that my dreams
      collecting below the promised aroma of cooking

won't chase me up and down the nightmare stairs.
   Nor that the day, outside the aura of the pot,
      won't be a dizzying examination

of that familiar nightscape. The handful of beans I toss into the water
   is good as any definition I know of future, noun seldom used
      in my childhood. *A time yet to be* where I find myself now

with a plan for a carrot, stalk of celery
   cup of onion, all of which I gather together
      anytime I hunger

for blackness, beauty matched
   by the recollection of that thickness on my tongue,
      scent of citrus. In an advance of optimism,

I hold my ingredients at the ready:
   that I have pushed my cart through the dense aisles
      of shelved food, that I have picked my way through

what is wilted, rejected what is not fresh;
   my prayer for the days to come,
      I repeat weekly. Food—not bags and boxes,

cellophane and ink—food: the rattle and heft
   of the still-hard beans in my palm; a few
      black beans to eat, to draw my mouth around.

This is where I stake my claim;
   I serve up the soup. Whoever enters
      will be fortified. In the same breath there is black bean,

there is future, there is nightmare,
   there's a pot on the stove
      to attend to when I wake.

Storm

They're calling for disaster
all the way to Puerto Rico
where shop owners crisscross
plate-glass windows
with masking tape, and home owners
board up and nail down every porthole
attracting collision
with the natural world. In Florida,
my mother-in-law worries the storm
will flash across that state
on the one night
in almost fifty years
she sleeps alone.

Hugo drapes its roily
black shadow over the housetops
of New England. The rigid bodies
of sunflowers circle the flower bed
in giant distress. Wrenched trees
drop from the sky
to land like ancient sticks of prophesy.

There are times I plan to live
more deliberately, to return
to small steps of caution,
and train my field of vision
on a fixed point in the universe.
Even knowing
what devastation reshapes the map—
the lightning rod that is
this solitary self—
I cannot stop myself.
I drive out into the storm in darkness.

Notes

"Love Poem to the Family" is for my aunt, Lillian Rotana.

"She Masters the Code" is for Lilian Fishman Kline.

"Study" is for Andrew Yeatman Kline.

The italicized lines in "Singing" are from Paul Simon's song "Me and Julio Down by the Schoolyard."

"Hearts" is for Janna Osman and Patty Morgan.

"Tableau with Beautiful Women and Weights" is for Kit Gates.

"An Ocean Between" is for Valentina Morse.

"Livno, Bosnia, 1994" is for Katica Jurendic.

"Winter Blooms" is for Rebecca Davison.

The title "Elderly Man Kills Wife, Self" was a headline from a local newspaper.

How to Order

To order a copy of *Drive*, please send a check or money order for $12.95 (Vermont residents add 5% sales tax) plus $3 for first-class postage and handling to

Brown Pepper Press
P.O. Box 1030
Montpelier, VT 05601

Drive was set in Palatino, a typeface designed by Hermann Zapf in 1948, and Optima, also designed by Zapf in 1952–55. It was printed on Glatfelter Eggshell by Capital City Press in Montpelier, Vermont.